3

THE OPPOSITE OF PEOPLE

Also by Patrick Ryan Frank

How the Losers Love What's Lost

THE OPPOSITE OF PEOPLE

Patrick Ryan Frank

Four Way Books
Tribeca

Please direct all inquiries to:
Editorial Office
Four Way Books
POB 535, Village Station
New York, NY 10014
www.fourwaybooks.com

Library of Congress Cataloging-in-Publication Data

Frank, Patrick Ryan.
[Poems. Selections]
The opposite of people / Patrick Ryan Frank.
pages ; cm
ISBN 978-1-935536-61-1 (softcover : acid-free paper)
I. Title.
PS3606.R384A6 2015
811'.6--dc23
2015006035

This book is manufactured in the United States of America and printed on acid-free paper.

Four Way Books is a not-for-profit literary press. We are grateful for the assistance
we receive from individual donors, public arts agencies, and private foundations.

NYSCA

This publication is made possible with public funds from the New York State Council on the Arts,
a state agency.

[clmp]

We are a proud member of the Community of Literary Magazines and Presses.

Distributed by University Press of New England
One Court Street, Lebanon, NH 03766

We're actors—we're the opposite of people.

—Tom Stoppard
Rosencrantz and Guildenstern Are Dead

CONTENTS

SILENT FILM

Soft light through leaves, two kids beside a car
flirting. You'll think of this after it ends,
after you watch the slapstick fade to war—

pilots, bullets, blood, and one last kiss
as death glides in on strings. The future lends
the past its battered light. Come back to this:

his hand along the roadster's chassis, the way
the engine stammers like a man who opens
his mouth before he knows what he has to say.

Day Time

THE GREAT AMERICAN SCREENPLAY

In corporate offices across the city,
in every company's cubicle-chambered heart,

there are men alone all lunch hour: men
who watch the tendons shifting in their hands

as they type *love* over and over again—
ring finger, ring finger, index, middle—softly,

though, only barely touching the keys,
never hard enough to light up the screen.

THE DAYS OF OUR LIVES

For most of each day all summer, we were no one—
just indoor boys with nothing much to do
but sit with sitters whose throats were as tight as ours
and let the television tell us what we wanted:

a blonde in a coma, her handsome husband wanted
for murder, his mysterious twin whom no one
had seen in years returned to a town like ours
with scores to settle and terrible things to do

to that old woman with a young girl's hairdo
and all that money. Everybody wanted
the money. We lusted through each afternoon
after sex and pretty trouble to fill the hours

that laid themselves out like a femme fatale. Ours
were lives of wrecks and feuds, and we would do
anything for someone who moaned they wanted
to show us danger where before there'd been none.

No one wondered what would be left to do
with all of it ours and almost what we wanted.

EX INGÉNUE

One weekend spent with a thin, blonde spinster aunt,
with her tulip-covered sofa, chocolates, her cough
as she talked through war films with the sound turned off,
her half-sung sayings: *if you got what you want,*
no one would know you anymore. Her laughter
was low and long, a smolder when I left her
to another summer smoking on the lawn
in a faded orange bathing suit and tan lines,
watching for the mailman at the gate—
hers was the patient glory of the landmine
waiting for a foot's right weight.

COMMERCIAL FOR A WEIGHT-LOSS PLAN

The blurred *before*, awful and ill-lit,
and then the *after*, bright as a champagne flute,
but never a picture of the miserable middle:
the hunger and the scale, the weights and sweat,
the swearing of a girl who kicks the slow
untrained dog of her body, then feels bad
and feeds it every sweet scrap she can find.
How does anyone not hate the thing
they know will make them happy? Hide those photos.
Let no one ever know how hard it was,
that want so starved it gnawed itself apart.

AS IN A FILM, TWO LOVERS

Poplar. Maple with its bleeding bark.
She leads him down the path, naming trees

while a drum corps rumbles somewhere near.
First day of summer; they've just met—a glance

on the street, chance smile among the people there
waiting for a parade to start. He thinks

his ribs would break apart if she touched the skin
below his ear, just briefly, barely, once.

She can't believe how pale his eyelids are
in the shivered jigsaw shadows of the leaves,

or that this is really how it all begins:
a drumroll, a drumroll, and then the horns break in.

PATRICK RYAN FRANK AS THE INFORMANT

Smaller than all the things I'd never done,
I went unnoticed. But then that Russian's death
and I was asked about the stolen guns,
the cocaine and the meth, and all that happened
happened again in my high whisper, clear
as vodka in an offered glass. Full
of names, connections, I couldn't stop, felt then
as if a red bird lived inside my mouth—
we sang together from our tall stool
and men in gray suits held their breath to hear.

AND EACH IN THE CELL OF HIMSELF

In Memory of the Marlboro Man

A man might see a certain shade or shape
of mustache or an unexpected hat
and be knocked back, thinking of nothing more
than lying down right there and waking up
to a cloudy morning in 1978,
a man's voice through a thin wall calling, *Oh,
Carmello*, as a record plays in the dark
of a basement, the party already started or
still going and it just won't end, and parked
across the street is the big white car—no,
the small red truck—that is going to take you back,
still almost convinced of your freedom, to the fields
and fall-down chicken coops where everyone knows
that you belong but you, holding the fag
to your lips, posing against the highway rail,
thinking, *This is me. Yes, this is real.*

MAKEOVER

I'm only this, and this is not enough.
Because each body is an accident.
Because my body is the opposite

of mystery, and yet I cannot solve
myself. I will not know until I'm shown.
Because I want to step into a life

as a wealthy woman steps into a store.
Because the fountain's full of coins already,
and the escalator doesn't pause its glide

upward into grace. I will be more
than what I seem. My heels on the marble floor
will sound like every door in hell thrown wide.

COMMERCIAL FOR A PERSONAL-INJURY LAWYER

Careless driver, careless doctor—now
it hurts, you're out of work, it's someone's fault.
I'll find out whose and make them hear you say
the words *I deserve.* A smart man knows
that justice is just discovering what your pain
is worth. It's a number you can grit
between your teeth as you twist in bed at night.
You'll write it on every slip of paper: all
those zeroes lined up like the open *Ohs*
of their mouths as they, at last, remember your name.

PATRICK RYAN FRANK AS THE DETECTIVE

Face as grim as an evidence locker full
of guns and white-tagged plastic bags of drugs,
knives and ripped-up clothes, lengths of rope.
It's all that's left of a life of knowing too much

about malice and mistakes. Just watch a man
long enough and you'll learn a thing or two
about yourself. Not the obvious—
that you are not so different; no one is—

but that you've come to love the awful things
that others do. Not just the *how* or *who*
or *why*, but the battered body in its pile.
You'll see me at the scene while the blood's still wet.

I won't be smiling, stepping through the glass,
but I might mumble *not me, not me, not yet.*

THIS MUST BE THE PLACE

Autumn, a rental, a radio, and a map—
another man excuses himself from the highway
to look for the actual world: a tourist trap,
a town that hasn't had its trigger pulled,
those pretty girls about to fly away.
It eats at you, the fear that you've been fooled
into believing what you have is real,
quietly asking the movies how to feel.
You understand why your grandparents spent
their decades with that television set,
polished wood and full of weather: snowstorm,
snowstorm, static through the night.
Watch it long enough, it must be life.
Somewhere, a man casually loves his wife;
a woman sitting on her sofa says,
goddamn or *hallelujah* or *not today*;
and somewhere near, the deer and foxes do
what deer and foxes do, unseen, unknown.
Someone who looks like you drives into town.
Nothing special: some stores and a bar or two,
kids in the park beside the Eagles Hall,
old women enjoying the last of this weather, warm
as the wind picks up and the red leaves start to fall.

FUNNY KID

About violence they were never wrong,

the old cartoons: there was always a fist
becoming a punch, always someone to twist

his arm behind his back. But no one rescued
anybody else; he wasn't strong
or fast, and what was he supposed to do?

The animated soldiers had their guns,
the animals had magic or whatever,
but he had nothing, so he had to be clever.
He knew the one wrong thing in everyone

could be found out, sharpened, flashed out like a blade.
Bad teeth, drunk mother on welfare—it felt a little
like touching a bruise as it begins to fade,
odd but good, standing in the middle
of everybody laughing and afraid.

ANTI-DEPRESSANT COMMERCIAL

Clear sky except a cloud much like a face
of a pretty girl who pretended to be sad
so long that now she's sad. Sad cloud, the sun

runs its fingers through everybody's curls
but pulls back when it gets to yours. Your rain
is falling nowhere else. No one likes

wet hair or umbrellas; no one likes
you. A meteorologist once lay flat
beneath you, open-mouthed, and that was sweet

but brief, and that was all, and that was that.
So what? Now what? The wind's died down and you
go nowhere, just stay awkwardly in your dark

part of the garden. Men with cameras talk
about you, saying it isn't all that hard,
just count to five, then turn, pretend to smile.

AFTER THE BREAK

Almost five months, no job, it falls apart:
the bills all due, the money's running out,
but everything is coming out okay
across the cooking shows, makeover shows,
the home-improvement shows where a man stands up
his ladder like a capital letter, an *A*
that stands for anything. For anything?
For another afternoon and all of that?

YOUR HIGH-SCHOOL SWEETHEART
MAKES ANOTHER PROMISE

One day, I won't get drunk. I'll pick you up
in a borrowed pickup truck and take you back
to that Dairy Queen downtown and then the park,
the playground, dugout. We'll smoke; I'll do those jokes
again, but better. I'll let you have the rest
of my chocolate, and I'll listen when you talk
about your father, gone; the others, gone.
And when the sun goes finally down, we'll buy
a lotto ticket at every liquor store
to the county line. I'll show you I can drive
as fast as luck and drums in dumb pop songs
down those black back roads, gravel and long.
And if we swerve and end up in a ditch,
I'll give you my jacket and we'll shuffle back
and I will tell you why the years fell out
that way. You'll say, *we're not eighteen*. I'll say,
that's why it's going to work this time. We'll walk
along the center line, the yellow dashes
between us, all of it how you always wanted.
There will be crickets and some nightbirds, yes.
Of course, familiar stars. Of course, the moon
as small and hard as candy or a baseball
knocked across an empty outfield. You'll see—
it'll be better than you ever thought:
you and me in all that darkness, then
a slow car coming, lighting up the trees.

Prime Time

WE LIVED AS IF BY SCRIPT AND CUE

But quietly, then, what went so wrong went wrong.
The door stayed closed; the phone lay there unrung.
What should have happened didn't, and the spoiled
minute tilted forward, fell, and we
were standing there as if a camera pulled
roughly back so everyone could see
the three unceilinged walls, the black around,
and us with nothing to say into the sound
of no one laughing, long and very loud.

THE COMEDIAN TAKES THE STAGE

Ever notice how a frightened man
will sway like an inflatable snowman tied
to some store's roof? No, neither have I.
It's surprisingly cold up here. See how my hands
are shaking? Someone told me to imagine you
all naked, which is harder than you'd think.
I told you that to break the ice, but it's true,
your bodies are strange. Maybe it's time for a joke.
Three men were walking down the street. . . Or two?
Was it two men walking? Two men were walking
down the. . . No, there was just one man talking
to nobody. It's all gone wrong, so let's
just say the ice is broken. As you sit
there so quietly, naked in my mind,
as naked as you are in the bath, in the dark
of your homes and your hotels, please be kind
enough to remember that I am trying hard
to press on, to push my way through this. Oh, wait—
was I supposed to be the naked one?
Are you all imagining me undressed? Do that,
I guess, while I figure out what comes next.
I wish I'd brought some props, a guitar, something
hysterical to show you, but I don't sing
and I'm up here empty-handed. No magic tricks
or video clips, no slides, no pictures of me
as a kid or drunk. I'm sorry for the lack
of funny pictures. Just imagine one:
a man in the water, naked maybe, under
the water and it's winter, there's ice, and he's

26

under the ice, he's hitting the ice with his fists,
hoping someone will hear and come to help.
Imagine there's only a sound like wind on plastic
and a far-off muffled guitar. Imagine his lips
are blue and his mouth is open and he has
this look in his eyes as he looks right at you, like
he sees you too. Imagine that as I back
slowly away from this microphone, these lights.
Goodnight, ladies. Gentlemen, goodnight.

ACTION / ADVENTURE

The office tower was glass. Now it's fire.
The villain and his henchmen speed through town
with one unkillable cop chasing them down
on a comically commandeered red scooter. Here

the flames are throwing a party in a wrecked
insurance office, making their bright confetti
from claims and actuary charts. Already,
the desktop family pictures have curled to black

ashes falling like pollen on the street
where an adjuster watches his job burn up. Bullet
dodged! An unexpected blessing! He feels it
in his ribcage—he survived so he could start

living beyond that awful office, spend
his days with his wife, see exotic places,
be important. He breathes the air that tastes
like freedom but is filled with dust that will end

up brooding in his lungs. He'll be dead
in a year: no decades of sex and hobbies, no
comfortable old age, no chance to show
a grandchild or some clever neighbor kid

his garden with its lilies and its ants,
its pretty weeds—so many tiny things
in a complicated world where anything
can happen, where it always, easily, can't.

CAR COMMERCIAL

Blue air, black road, red dirt, white car: white coupe
on its straight shot through a cloudless desert, fast
and bright and beautifully framed, metonymy
of a lovely life—spotless, stopless, smooth
unlyricked music and the quickest route
out of monotony and toward the curves
of Montana, its mountains grand as majesty
and breasts unconquered, or toward Manhattan, sleek,
still buildings serious, direct, reflected in
the windows, black so anybody could
be driving, even you, probably you
saying goodbye, dull bungalow, goodbye,
hello A/C, combustion brogue, the road
implausibly empty, flat, implausible sky.

THE GUN IN THE FIRST ACT

It came home in his briefcase. He showed her its clip,
the trigger and the safety, the proper grip.

It wasn't as she'd expected: not cold or dull.
It shined, hot in her hand, surprisingly small,

both delicate and heavy, like a baby
that didn't cry. It could fit in her pocket. Maybe

she'd carry it out sometimes, she said, in case. . .
He said he'd rather she left it in its place

in the nightstand drawer. They'd probably never need it,
but there's no harm in being prepared. She didn't

say anything, just aimed at the radio,
which sang to itself a song he didn't know.

THE COMEDIAN FALLS OFF THE WAGON

A guy walks into a bar and lifts a drink.
The light gets soft, the music picks right up,
and all my stupid jokes are suddenly
funny, the punch lines falling into place
like bright new quarters in the slot of a payphone
that no one's thought to use in years. I make
new friends and tell them every single thing—
the stars I've met, sure-bet investments, that girl
who washed her hair in my tears all those years
ago—and then I whirl out into the street,
alone in the smooth black early hours of morning.
It isn't lonely, or if it's lonely, it's lovely
like a movie. I feel as real and ready
as a nine-volt battery, so full of thrill
and set to go. But then the light goes dull
and the empty street is just an empty street
and quiet again. But still, still then, something
still might happen, someplace open still,
someone and just one more, that's it, another.

PATRICK RYAN FRANK AS THE OTHER WOMAN

Plagiarist of feelings, fooling around
in a dark car parked in the snow outside the fence
of a nowhere airfield. Curious, mostly. More
than anything else, I want to know what it's like
to be that figure there in the heater dust
and rustle, runway strobes lighting up
the hair and hands, the jacket buttons. And words—
half planned-ahead and pretty, meaning something
somehow different in that setting, as when
I moan, *I cannot be alone right now,*
I mean, *let me be not myself for once,*
let me be thrilled and thrilling, show me how.

STUNT MAN

Sheathed in flames and screaming down the street,
I realized how much I've come to hate
the world. I'm always almost leaving it.

A harness holds me back: the practiced tackle,
crash, the sudden gravel, sudden glass,
and life is as dull as a propman's plastic knife.

The sky is just a space I've fallen through.
The sea is just another speedboat chase
waiting for the blast. Some people do

their dangerous acts to prove that they're alive.
I'm not like that. It's not my fault the world
keeps dreaming up new ways that I won't die.

THE COMEDIAN AT A FUNERAL

I've seen this movie; I know how I should act:
politely quiet, distracted by my grief.
But grief's an act I haven't mastered yet.
In fact, I'm almost happy. Everything
is hilarious and everything is wrong:
an awkward hand on the back, the mother's hat,
the sister's low-cut dress. Her body bends
toward the body in its odd white casket
and I wonder what if somehow this
is the only hour of my life that I
will not be sad. Living is just a joke
that no one gets, and I can't get it right.
Some bad-breathed aunt leans over, asks me how
I'm holding up, but there's lipstick on her teeth.
When I open my mouth, the wrong sound falls right out.

THE TROUBLE WITH BLONDES
IS THAT THEY'RE ALWAYS IN TROUBLE

Girls running up the stairs in lovely shoes.
Girls dancing slowly through those sunlit rooms
while someone outside stares. Unfair or not,
the world wraps all of its idiot pity around
the necks of all the pretty girls and pulls
them forward into that briefly gorgeous light.
A young girl builds a castle on the beach.
It's perfect, but the tide is coming in
so quickly that you can't feel all that bad
breaking it apart beneath your heel.

PATRICK RYAN FRANK AS THE RUSSIAN

The empire falls on him like snow in an orchard;
everything goes strange and stiffly white.
He wanders cities made burlesque with money
and music and the howling vagrant dogs.
He is a soldier in his Cossack boots
or a pale, blonde woman selling cigarettes.
Often, he's a boy, working alone
in a vast, half-fallow field, almost lost,
and there's a sky like the back of a jigsaw puzzle.
He's sure that in the distance, it all comes clear,
but here it's about to storm. A rust-red bird
is crowing a time that no one wants to hear.

THERE'LL BE AN ENORMOUS PARTY

Tumbling down that wide Niagara of laughter,
the blonde girls and the gray-haired men beside them
swirl away through picture after picture.
If there's champagne, there'll be a waiter's smirk.
If there's an ice sculpture, it will be a swan
weeping for its flaws. If there's a pool,
a horrible beautiful woman will end up pushed
and the garden will quiet just to hear her thrash
within the weird slick of her ruined silk—
and then the jokes and it all begins again.
Oh vanity, why won't you leave me home?
Why must you pull me by the elbow down
that crowded hallway then leave me by the wall,
awkward as an interrupted joke,
adrift in the back of half the photographs:
a face turned too far left, mouth spread too wide
to grin, gaping as if to gulp back breath?

PERFUME COMMERCIAL

Dear, I'd be the stark white night bloom blooming
and not some animal rustling through the brush
beneath and to the side. Not those wide eyes
reflecting the candle loosely held in your hand.
But no, I'd be that candle, thin and wax
and ready to melt, my suddenly stunning hair
blown back and bright like flame in a constant draft.
Or would that make me smoke? Pleasant and dark,
but brief, then gone—oh god, why do I drift
like this, over the pretty moonlit heads
of you and your well-coifed smooth-skinned love, your hands
on hips and chins and holding hard that lust
and practiced utter focus, as if you didn't see
the churning sea and distant city, or know
how perfectly you've been posed against the rail
of this salt-sprayed terrace with this moon
and these unnecessary candelabras
and night blooms blooming and, dammit, this animal
pacing, lifting its black nose to the wind.

MARILYN MONROE AND TRUMAN CAPOTE DANCE

El Morocco, New York, 1955

Darling, let's forget the details, dull
as they always are: who's here and not, the room

as hot as breath, and the orchestra lisping through
another number about love and harmless fun.

Let's someday remember it better, romantically vague.
Let's say I wanted to dance and so did you,

not pressed by the others together, no picture taken
of us spun drunken out from what's behind

our looks and jokes and what is said, the sum
of all this goddamn work. Just a dance—

just sweet, like everybody sweetly else,
a man and woman sweetly moved. I know

no one forgets the ugly things they've known,
and yes, I know that love, for us, is sweat

and panic and some cameras, but it's still love,
and we've done nothing wrong. So let them laugh

and then forget it all: those drinks and pills,
hands wet, that man who, grinning, made us dance

so here we are, we're dancing. Let's just pretend
that one of us—who would remember who?—

slipped through the grand and glittered dark and said,
Hello, fella. Hello and take my hand.

REPORTER

Impossible to cross a bridge without
imagining its collapse: which words he'd use
for the sound of the concrete cracking, for the cars
as they roll, the splintered glass exact in the sun,
the perfect details and their order, tone,
narrative of disaster. He slips from phrase
to phrase—*suspension cables snapped; the desperate
rescue workers*—as the river mumbles on
and cars press forward around him, every sentence
rising from the depths of a terrible joy.

THE COMEDIAN CONSIDERS

Nothing is funnier than unhappiness,
wrote Samuel Beckett, that bucket of ugly laughter.
And Kierkegaard once said that a person has
to suffer to know what's comic. Is that what I'm after,
a setup? Bad life lived badly so that when
the punch line comes it comes as a punch to the gut?
Can I work these cruelties and the accidents
into the perfect joke? And if so, so what?
I tell myself the funniest man in the world
lives in some village surrounded by bamboo
and wasps and hungry soldiers. When he's dead,
no one outside his valley will have heard
his laugh or the only English words he knew:
I'm sorry and *That's what your mama said.*

PROJECTIONIST

There is nothing that I cannot show you,
no face nor body, hour of any day,
no place too far or strange for me to reveal
among the permutations of my light,
penumbras, focus, and the turning reel.
Though we will never meet, I will know you
when you settle in your seat and the fugitives hide
and a green car idles in an alleyway,
while always I in my Plutonic dark—
unknown, unknowingly beloved—work
lavishly my magic with my lamp
and lens and spool. Look, the lovers linger
on a hushed side street. Look, the enemy camp.
And here you are, rushing between my fingers.

Late Night

MIDNIGHT COWBOY

The two men sitting in the coppered dark
of the skin-flick theater know their knees will touch.

And then? An empty wallet at your hip
will only buy a lonely night. And this

is the awkward, desperate truth of sex and cash:
without some, you can't get some; without any,

you die. The student leans in, tightens his lips
as if to whisper. Not, *I don't have that much,*

or, *I've never done this.* A joke, maybe, to make
it easy, *Do they make you join a union?*

The hustler watches while the actress drags
her fingernails across the actor's ass

and moans. The student knows you just can't say
you understand how everybody suffers

inside their bodies' idiotic hunger,
so he reaches for the hustler's fly

while the actress, thrown down on her back,
begs. The hustler has to close his eyes.

BODY DOUBLE

Bare and always my face is bent away.
I am modest and half-seen. My skin may

be laid there on the screen, but I stay vague
as sex or laughter half heard through a wall.

Maybe you think I'm all imposture, false
and empty semblance. So what? When I was young,

I played a game called *Radio*. Black sack
over my head, I'd open my mouth to sing.

I could be anybody in the dark,
and anybody could be listening.

MISS CLEO CAN HELP

Bad times. A birthmarked man. A broke-down car.
I see it all: the cards laid out, the stars
laid out in lines. I'll tell you what they mean
while the TV frame gets smaller and my face,
resigned like someone's mother, fills the screen,
as if you, with every right word that I say,
were coming closer. What do you want to hear?
The money's coming. The baby's daddy's gone.
You'll be alright if you just get over that fear
that everything you want is obvious
to everyone else. Honey, yes, I know
you wonder if you'll find true love. Right here,
you'll see it in my turban's folds, my cards—
I have such love, whatever the question: what place
or long-gone lover. It's so ridiculous,
it must be real. Ask about tomorrow,
the lotto; ask me, *where's my sister now?*
I'll ask you, *where am I?* Sweetheart, close
your eyes and find me: Florida prison cell
or selling handbags outside Syracuse.
Or in a jungle, casting off my clothes
and spinning, crazy as a carousel,
while all your sweethearts' ghosts begin to moan
and the night beats with the sound of the devil's heart.
Or in a plain brown room in a purple gown,

leaning over a desk, my hand held hard
above the phone like a thunderhead in drought,
dark and ready to open. Call me now.
I'll tell you how it is, how it all comes out.

MY WAY

A man in Manila is killed for singing Sinatra
off-key in a smoke-filled karaoke club.
It isn't the first time some happily half-drunk tough

opened his mouth and another pulled out a gun
or a knife and everybody's good time went bad.
And I understand. I've never hit a man

but there've been many men at bars and parties
who've spilled their drinks or laughed too loud or said
the wrong thing or haven't said anything at all.

The fist pulls itself. The fingers bend
into the pretty idiotic mouths.
I want to show everyone how it should be done

so hard that most of the time I have to hold
my body tightly still, a back-up singer
on a hazy stage, waiting for the beat.

PATRICK RYAN FRANK AS THE ASTRONAUT

After lift-off, the freedom of the limbs
from their glum weight, after congratulations
but before that whirring signal from
the fast-approaching asteroid, the klaxons
and the flashing lights and all that will happen after,
there's just this silence and unstartled black
beyond the shuttle's plastic porthole. There
is the planet, round and blue as a gumball hard
in some boy's sweating hand. How can this
be real? Nothing left to do but stare
at every single thing he's thought he's known
now so small it must all be unimportant—
old men skating, sailors in the ports,
a blond child choking in a parking lot—
if it can be right there and be unseen.
Lit by the flickering screens and already done
with the differences between what is and isn't,
he waits for what comes next, for what must come,
knowing at last it doesn't matter much
whether someone watches, someone listens.

COMMERCIAL FOR A PHONE-SEX HOTLINE

We're in a doctor's office and I'm a nurse.
Or you're a cop, or we both study math.
This is the township of satisfaction and you
are a registered voter. What would you like me to say?
That I'm wearing nothing but a collar and
we'll screw the way a late-night preacher works
his pews—there'll be music, there'll be wrath?
And shame is the clean white napkin a hungry man
will spread across his lap. And nothing has
to be its boring self anymore.
You'll be the bashful Latvian masseuse
and I'll be you, lying on the floor
in the dark with all those possibilities
and a touch-tone phone, knowing what to do
and knowing the truth: that once you pull yourself past
the stubborn body, the heart is so easy to please.

MODERN HORROR

Why a monster, why a man with a knife,
when the mailbox coughs up panic and the phone
is growling like a rabid dog? The bills,
bad news and test results, the dread red eye
of the IRS. I don't want to know what's next,
what's in my house already. I've run upstairs
to the inescapable attic of my life
wearing my highest heels. I've turned my back
to the hungry dark of the opening closet door,
to the vague black shapes on the floor. Here's a window
and it's still a lovely night, with wind in the trees
and shadows like people running, light like fires
breaking out in houses down the street.

FUNNY OLD MAN

His old age came on quickly: a roar in his ears,
low and distant, like an audience yelling
when the star walks off. Soon, he couldn't hear
anything but himself, but he kept telling
his jokes, until they started to disappear—

just the first half, all the setups; he held
hold of every punch line he'd ever told,
while everything else walked out: faces and old
grudges, slurs and binges. At first, he felt

he'd been put in the cheap last row of his life, the stage
too far away to see the comic's smirk,
to follow all that intricate empty rage,

to know that the night-shift nurses on their rounds
walked slower past his room to hear the sound—

some mumbling and soft laughter in the dark.

AS IN A FILM, TWO LOVERS

The dog on its tether lopes around the pole,
tracing in the dirt a tightening circle.

Night comes. Inside, a man and woman sit
across a kitchen table. He smokes, she sips

her wine from a plastic cup. A radio hums
somewhere. He thinks she'd kill him if she could.

She thinks the same. Soon, they'll go upstairs;
they'll fuck, then fall asleep. But now, as the room

gets darker, she sees less and less of him,
and finally just the tip of his cigarette,

that orange spark that lifts and dims and flares.

PATRICK RYAN FRANK AS THE ALIEN

At last revealed. At last himself. A thing
stepping, unsteadily as a patient, out
of his skin disguise and into the honest light.
No talons and no tail, no wasp-thin wings,
a body odd but oddly familiar, mouth
reddened on the hairless head, teeth
clicking together around that theramin voice.
The hero lifts his fists and won't be menaced.
Disgusted, the heroine screams but is not scared.
Even the creature with his many plans
knows that nothing's going to turn out right,
and he wonders what was the point of all of this—
the women running blindly, scientists grim,
the soldiers silent behind their guns. No one
lives beyond the planet of himself.
Tomorrow, the square-jawed captain will marry his girl,
and then they'll fight. The bankers will count their bills;
newspapers will print the pages that will drift
across a lot that was a crash site once,
its alien gone, melted down to nothing
with a sound like people talking all at once
about nothing important as the lights come up
and they move toward the daylight through the door.

COMMERCIAL FOR CAR INSURANCE

A man in the driver's seat with a sweet half-smile
that lets you know that every day there's less

reason not to lift his hands from the wheel
and let the tires take him where they'll go.

How far could he get before some broke-down truck
or just a curve ahead, out of luck

and into a thicket of homemade roadside crosses?
Someone who sees how easy it is to let

it all go wrong, even when he knows
he still has a little time to turn it right,

and maybe he would if he weren't so curious
to see what happens, if it's true when they say

everything is going to be okay.

TIME IS A CAR WITH ITS BRAKE LINES CUT

And everybody on the screen is dead—
the waiter and the charming, sinister rogue

and the already-old old lady, even the lovers,
Gary Cooper and Marlene Dietrich,

lustrous in the monochromatic light
of *Desire*, a hit from 1936,

the last quick days a blonde on the run in Spain
could find herself facing nothing worse

than a tall American opening his coupe
to carry her around the curves and cliffs

toward a decent happy ending where
they, the jeweler, the comic doctor laugh

their way to those off-screen years, unseen and quick
with cancer and the hearts' red bells rung out.

I've never understood what's wrong with me,
looking for melancholy in the jokes

and pretty sets where probably there was none.
Dietrich and Cooper were clearly having fun

and an affair, as trivial and nice
as a back-lot comedy, easy because

they were comfortably famous, gorgeous, thirty-five,
which, in those early years before the movies

taught us better, seemed still young. Still time,
they must have thought, at least a little left,

to be unworried, another starlit kiss
on the terrace, another cognac. . . Then, a curve:

Franco's coup and war, the world in halves
and Spain the pivot, that scenic village bombed,

the villa burned, black and bullet-pocked
that terrace. Time speeds and time is speeding up.

The tanks roll into Poland, then to Paris;
Pearl Harbor happens and the parts get thin:

soldier, sheriff, soldier—Cooper holds
tightly to his gun, the way he thinks

a good man would. Dietrich sings "God Bless
America" in her German accent near

the German lines, close enough to see
her homeland fall apart. And then the bomb,

but nothing's over. Cold War, Korean War,
the record skip of war, quick as the lines

on the highway disappearing beneath the wheel,
and everyone is old. The hero still

and always, still busy, Cooper rumbles through
his Westerns, grin gone thin, then gone, and still

the handsome cowboys coming younger and younger
to the set, laughing with their starlets, small

as insults. What do they know? What have they done
but grow up quickly, loosely, and good-looking?

Dietrich must have also understood
the way the landscape shifts so quickly, as when

in Berlin, on the street where she was born,
a crowd of widows and former soldiers shouted

TRAITOR, held up signs that said *GO HOME!*
And where is that? It's 1954

and London, a nightclub's flowered dressing room
with all its mirrors, and, in each, her face.

Gray face, all bruise and wither, still her face,
and that's the awful thing. Better to see

a stranger there, unknown, unrecognized,
than find again those eyes, still hard and bright

when everything else goes dull and soft and wrong.
Why can't we fade into someone else?

People wait in lines outside to watch
her as she was: hard angel; cold, white flame

of the matinee. That's what they've paid to see.
So here she sits at a table laid with makeup

and a sewing kit. Her mother taught her how
to thread a needle, that the eye is small

but still a little larger than the thread,
and easily it's done and ready. She looks

at the bird-nest wrinkles in the mirror, lines
around her mouth like cracks in ice and tries

to imagine it's another person there,
as when that soldier at the German border

asked her for her name (pretending not
to recognize that face), she thought to say,

Maria Magdalene, whom she'd be
if she had stayed some sweet small nobody.

She pulls the skin below her temple back
until the wrinkles smooth, the cheekbones surface,

sharp again. The needle pierces the fold,
the thread runs red with blood as she pulls it through.

Her makeup and the wig will cover it
completely. Stitch after stitch, the predator flight

of the needle pauses only long enough
for her to pull the jaw a little tighter,

to smooth her cheek and tie the small, hard knot
that has to hold through half a dozen songs.

It's awful, the awful detail and what I've done—
plucked it out and lingered over it,

as if one moment could reveal some grief
at the center of a long, odd life. I know

that just because it's terrible doesn't mean
it means a thing. But I'm writing it here

because I understand how it feels
to look into a mirror and see yourself

unlike yourself—new frown lines, thinning hair,
slack cheeks and unsmooth skin, and still it's me—

to feel time rushing on, while always square
in the middle of that terrifying looking

forward into open air, there's
a rearview mirror. Tomorrow, I'll be less

handsome than I am today, which is less
than I was ten years ago—no Gary Cooper,

no, but an eager kid comfortable in
his skin without its blotches and its aches,

not yet obsessed with these indignities.
I know it's vanity but I'm thirty-four

and I'm afraid of being old and full
of cancer, disappointment. I don't want

to slowly die like Cooper: crumpled wreck
of flesh and tubes, mumbling in his bed

about the work to do, the parts he'll play,
while people quietly sit around and watch

death in its performance. I don't want
to live like Marlene Dietrich: holding tight

to her gone looks with costumes, lighting, booze
and pills, becoming glamorously grotesque.

At least, at last, she gave up and withdrew
into her mystique and her Paris flat,

refusing to be seen after decades
of nothing else. Finally—fully—old,

she became her pictures and her songs,
a voice on the phone, unchanged, unchangeable,

then died, unviewed and happily alone,
when I was ten. I'd never heard of her

or seen her films. I didn't understand
nostalgia yet. I didn't know I would.

Or that I'd someday lean against a car
and be kissed, and someday later that would be

the moment in my mind when I was young
and in control of where my life was going.

Toward the end, Marlene Dietrich wrote
that *Desire* was the only film she'd made

of which she didn't need to be ashamed.
Her thief is beautiful and effortless;

Cooper's mechanic has an easy laugh;
and when the moonlight presses them together,

their kiss goes on and on. It doesn't matter
what will come because it's not here yet.

Desire is not for someone but for when—
right place, right light, one look, the slow embrace

(Hold—and cut!) and I can understand
how even while the landmarks of her years

grew smaller in the mirror, she still loved
this fiction, a pretty little ninety minutes,

sweet and unimportant. No one gets hurt
and all the trouble's past with none ahead.

This is how the movie of my life
should end: sunlight through a slender tree

above a car's white hood. A siren fades.
Someone laughs. Someone says my name.

NOTES

"Silent Film": *Wings* (dir. William A. Wellman) won the first Academy Award for Best Picture, then referred to as the Most Outstanding Production.

"The Days of Our Lives": The titular soap opera has aired nearly every weekday since November 8, 1965.

"And Each in the Cell of Himself": The title is taken from a line in W. H. Auden's "In Memory of W. B. Yeats."

"The Gun in the First Act": The title is from a gloss of an adage attributed to Anton Chekhov: if a gun appears in the first act, it has to be fired in the third.

"Marilyn Monroe and Truman Capote Dance": This poem was inspired by Garry Winogrand's photographs of Capote and Monroe dancing.

"My Way": According to the *New York Times* (February 6, 2010), at least half a dozen people, possibly more, have been killed in the Philippines since 2001 because of disputes over karaoke renditions of the Frank Sinatra hit, "My Way."

"Midnight Cowboy": The Motion Picture Association of America gave *Midnight Cowboy* (dir. John Schlesinger) an X rating due to the movie's "homosexual frame of reference," particularly a scene in which Bob Balaban's character propositions John Voight's hustler in a porn theater. After the film won the Academy Award for Best Picture, becoming the only X-rated film ever to win an Oscar, the MPAA adjusted their requirements and retroactively gave *Midnight Cowboy* an R rating.

"Miss Cleo Can Help": Youree Dell Harris, claiming to be a Jamaican shaman, became famous as a television psychic and spokesperson for a pay-per-call hotline in the late 1990s and early 2000s. The companies she represented grossed an estimated five-hundred million dollars before being sued in over a dozen states for fraud and false advertising. The lawsuits were settled out of court. Harris disappeared from the public eye for many years, but has recently, as Miss Cleo, made several attempts at a comeback.

"Time is a Car with its Brake Lines Cut": *Desire* (dir. Frank Borzage) was filmed partially on location in France and pre-war Spain. It was the second, and final, feature film that Dietrich and Cooper made together. Gary Cooper died in 1961; Marlene Dietrich died in 1992.

ACKNOWLEDGMENTS

I would like to thank the editors of the following journals for originally publishing several of these poems: *American Literary Review, Barrow Street, Boxcar Poetry Review, Carolina Quarterly, Confrontation, Diagram, Failbetter, Georgetown Review, Green Hills Literary Lantern, The Harlequin, Mantis, New Ohio Review, North American Review, Poet Lore, Rattle, Shankpainter,* and *Slate.*

I appreciate all of the people who have helped me with this collection. The teachers and mentors who have weighed in on these poems include Mary Reufle, Tomaž Šalamun, and Dean Young. Without intending to, A. Van Jordan and Robert Pinsky each gave advice that contributed to the genesis of this book. This project was supported by the Fulbright Program, the James A. Michener Center for Writers, the Kimmel Harding Nelson Center for the Arts, and the Woodstock Byrdcliffe Guild; the staff and the other artists at those programs have had a profound effect on my work. I have to thank my editor, Martha Rhodes, for her indulgence, as well as all of the fantastic staff at Four Way Books. And I'm especially grateful for Lawrence Kaplun and Andrew Rawson, two good friends and great readers, who gave early drafts of this manuscript an amazing measure of care and attention, and Justin Karas, who found the book's true face.

Like every writer, I am deeply indebted to my influences, particularly the poems, movies, television shows, songs, and real people referenced, directly or not, in this book. It is with great respect and admiration that I invoke them.

Patrick Ryan Frank's previous collection of poems, *How the Losers Love What's Lost*, won the 2010 Four Way Books Intro Prize for Poetry. Educated at Northwestern University, Boston University, and the James A. Michener Center for Writers at the University of Texas at Austin, he was twice a fellow at the Fine Arts Work Center in Provincetown, Massachusetts, and a recent Fulbright grantee to Iceland. He grew up in front of a television set in rural Michigan.